JIM
who ran away from his Nurse and was eaten BY a LION

HILAIRE BELLOC

AND piCTURES BY MiNi GrEY

RED FOX

There was a Boy

whose name was Jim;

Early to bed
and early to rise
makes a boy
healthy, wealthy
and quieter than usual.

Children
should be
seen
and not
heard.

All good things
must come
to an end.

RED FOX

UK | USA | Canada | Ireland | Australia
India | New Zealand | South Africa

Red Fox is part of the Penguin Random House group of companies
whose addresses can be found at global.penguinrandomhouse.com.

www.penguin.co.uk
www.puffin.co.uk
www.ladybird.co.uk

Penguin
Random House
UK

First published by Jonathan Cape, 2009
This Red Fox edition published 2017

002

Text copyright © The Estate of Hilaire Belloc, 1907, 2009
Illustrations copyright © Mini Grey, 2009

The moral right of the author and illustrator has been asserted

A CIP catalogue record for this book is available from the British Library

ISBN: 978–1–862–30875–6

All correspondence to:
Red Fox
Penguin Random House Children's UK: One Embassy Gardens,
8 Viaduct Gardens, London SW11 7BW

MIX
Paper from
responsible sources
FSC® C018179
www.fsc.org

His Friends were
very good to him.

They gave him Tea,

and Cakes,

and Jam,

And slices of delicious Ham,

And Chocolate
with pink
inside,

And little
Tricycles
to ride,
And

read him

Stories

through

and through,

And even took
him to the

But there it was the dreadful Fate Befell him, which I no...

ZOO RULES AND BYELAW

eep off the Grass t all times.

here will be no skipping, pping, ning or cavorting on Grass, and no king or picking of Grass.

Grass is the property e Zoo.

e will be no tree ing or balancing on

games are strictly bited.

ROHIBITED BSTANCES

substances are den within the Zoo ds:

Chewing Gum
Boiled Sweets
Sticky Drinks
eam   Frisbees

ng of French Cheese o the Zoo is **Forbidden.**

ur own risk.

sers will ecuted.

SIVE

hrieking

Low-pitched Noises

No humming, whistling or rustling.

No moaning, groaning, snorting or coughing.

No scratching, rubbing, picking or itching.

No sniffing, twitching or gulping.

No giggling, sniggering or chortling.

No silly voices.

Impersonating a Keeper or Animal is Forbidden.

ANNOYING WAYS OF EATING AND FORBIDDEN PACKAGING

No picnics.

No snacks.

No gargling, slurping, chomping or grinding.

No dribbling or nibbling.

The consuming of noisy foodstuffs in the Zoo is forbidden.

Strictly no rustly packaging especially risp Packets and Sweet appers.

eshments are to be med solely in the al Zoo Café on the ccasions it is open.

NT GESTURES

winking, blinking, ling, thumbing or p ng, especially at a Keep Animal.

No fun oks.

STRICT O PRACTIC KES.

STYLES OF D ESS

Zoo visitors shoul ess respectably.

Hats are to be worn.

Visitors must ensure eir underwear is clean t all times.

THESE ITEMS OF CLOTHING ARE IBITED:

uspenders
Loud ties
y shoes

M RES O M

loit
dayo
No
rushi
No hopping.
No singing or danc
Excitement of any sort is prohibited.

Visitors should maintain a brisk pace at all times and keep their hands to themselves.

THE ANIMALS

DO NOT FEED THE ANIMALS

Do not pet or stroke the animals.

Do not prod or poke the animals.

No taunting, jeering or teasing.

KEEP YOUR DISTANCE

IF YOU ARE AN ANIMAL:

No trumpeting
No stampeding
No charging
No constricting
No mauling
No circling
No swarming

IT'S YOUR OWN TIME YOU'RE WASTING

No squawking.
No spawning.
No stalking.
No migrating.
No grazing. No rutting.
No masticating.
No chirping. No nesting.
No preening.
No regurgitating.
No gnawing.

No hibernating.
No foraging. No buz
No purring. No grow
No chirruping.
No hooting. No too
squawking.

TLY NO ENTATIOU ATING DISPLAYS

GENERAL ZOO RU

No winking, blinking, drinking, stinking or thinking.

No clapping, slapping, napping, tapping, flapping, or yapping.

No yowling, howling, o prowling.

Don't try anything clev

Strictly No Fun And Games

USE YOUR HANDKERCHIE

WASH YOUR HANDS

PULL UP YOUR SOCK

DO AS YOU ARE TOLD

BRUSH YOUR TEET

BLOW YOUR NOSE

COMB YOUR HAI

DON'T TALK WITH YOUR MOUTH FULL

Not Too Fast
Careful Now
I wouldn't if I were you

AND FINALLY....

Look Before You Leap. Handsome is as handsome does. You cannot have your cake and eat it. The early bird catches the worm. Curiosity killed the cat. Let sleeping dogs lie. Fine words butter no parsnips. Better to be safe than sorry. Don't put all your eggs in one basket. You can't take it with you. Waste not want not. Leave well alone.

We told you so.

DO NOT STICK YOUR FINGERS THROUGH

Now this was Jim's especial Foible,
He ran away when he was able,

NO RUNNING

And on this inauspicious day
He slipped his hand and ran away!

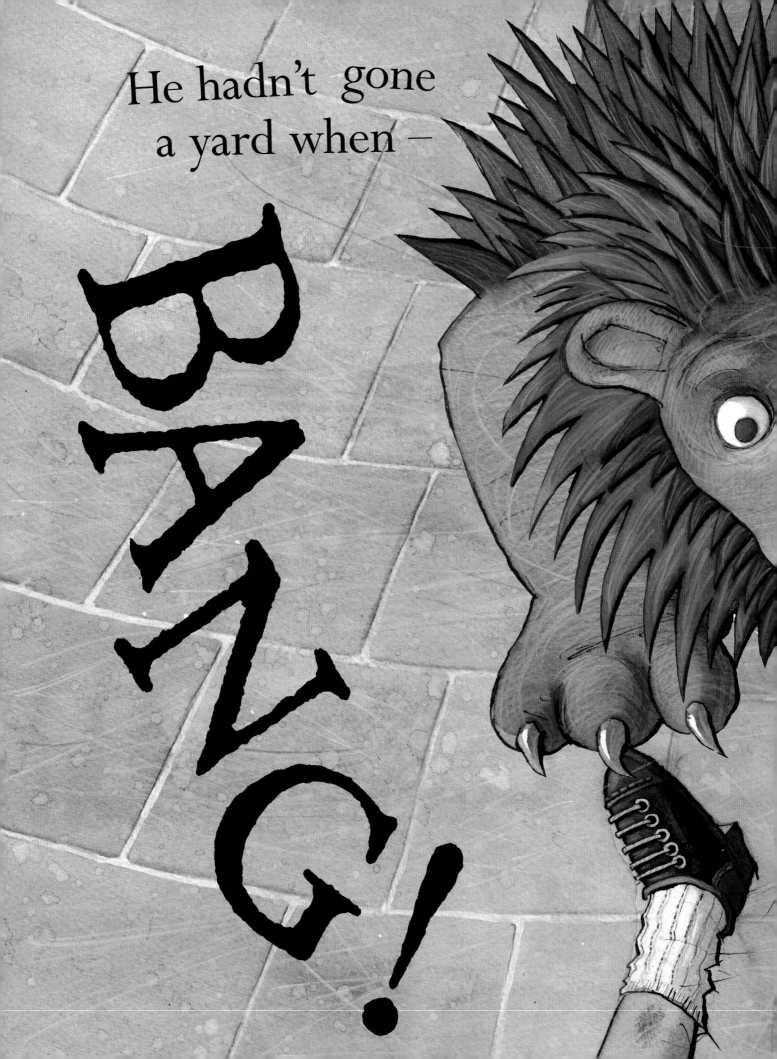

He hadn't gone
a yard when –

BANG!

With open Jaws,
a Lion sprang,

And
hungrily
began
to eat
The Boy:

beginning
at
his
feet.

NOW

JUST IMAGINE HOW IT FEELS

WHEN FIRST YOUR TOES

AND THEN YOUR HEELS

AND THEN BY GRADUAL DEGREES
YOUR SHINS AND ANKLES
CALVES AND KNEES

ARE SLOWLY EATEN BIT BY BIT.

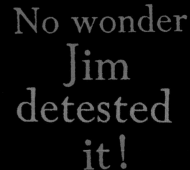

No wonder Jim detested it!

The Honest Keeper heard his cry,

Though very fat he almost ran
To help the little gentlemen.

The Lion made a sudden Stop,
He let the Dainty Morsel drop,

And slunk reluctant to his Cage,
Snarling with Disappointed Rage.

'Ponto!' he ordered as he came
(For Ponto was the Lion's name),

'Ponto!' he cried, with angry Frown.
'Let go, Sir! Down, Sir! Put it down!'

But when he bent him over Jim,
The Honest Keeper's Eyes were dim.

The Lion having reached his Head,
The Miserable Boy was dead!

strength to push with his
nst the beards behind, and had
eeded in gaining his liberty.
as he got into the street, a boy

neck. I was then of a more vigorous
frame than now, and had plenty of pluck
and dash in me.
I tried thus to stop h:

MY STRUGGLE WITH A TIGER.
IT is now a good many years ago, when
one morning a van-load of wild beasts
which I had bo

tiger, with its iron-barred front close
against the wall.
They were proceeding to take do
den with leopard

SATURDAY, FEBRUARY 1,
of about nine yea
hand to stroke

When Nurse informed his Parents, they
Were more Concerned
than I can say: —

His Mother, as She dried her eyes,
Said, 'Well — it gives me no surprise,
He would not do as he was told!'

His Father, who was
self-controlled,
bade all the children
round   attend
To   James'
              miserable
      end,

And always keep
a-hold of Nurse

For fear of finding s ome thing WORSE.

Children
should be
eaten
and not
heard.